F⬥CUS ⬥N

Writing Composition 1

Ray Barker   Louis Fidge

Nelson

	Stories with familiar settings	Plays	Myths, legends, fables, parables	Traditional stories	Adventure and mystery	Poems – observation and senses	Shape poems	Oral and performance poems	Humorous poems	Poetry with language play	Information texts	Non-chronological reports	Instructions	Letters	Recounts	Alphabetic texts
FICTION											**NON-FICTION**					
	✓															
	✓															
	✓			✓												
						✓		✓	✓							
							✓			✓						
		✓		✓												
											✓	✓				
												✓				
			✓	✓												
				✓												
			✓													
				✓												
								✓	✓							
													✓			
											✓					
	✓			✓												
				✓												
				✓								✓				
								✓	✓							
														✓		
															✓	
																✓

Contents

UNIT 1   Writing Dialogue

Think ahead

In a piece of writing, 'dialogue' is the words that are spoken when people have a conversation. When dialogue is included in stories it makes them more interesting. How can we tell from a piece of writing when anyone is speaking?

Rupinda brought her dirty plate into the kitchen and dumped it on the surface. She turned and started to walk back into the living room to watch the television.

"Just a minute," her dad said. "What about helping me first? You're not too busy to wash up, are you?"

"Sorry, Dad. Our washing-up liquid makes me come out in a rash," Rupinda answered.

"How about taking the rubbish out to the bin, then?" her father asked.

"I'm afraid I hurt my arm at school today. I think the bag would be too heavy," Rupinda replied.

"The living room needs cleaning. Try pushing the vacuum cleaner around. That will help your arm," suggested her father.

"You know I'm allergic to dust!" Rupinda responded immediately.

"What a pity you're not feeling up to much," Rupinda's dad said. "I was just going to suggest we went into town to buy you some new trainers!"

Thinking back

1 Write the conversation between Rupinda and her father as a playscript. When a new person speaks, start a new line like this:

   Dad   Just a minute. What about helping me first?
            You're not too busy to wash up are you?

2 Write what you think Rupinda said to her father at the end.

Thinking about it

1 Copy the dialogue below between Rupinda and her mother. Put speech marks in the correct places.

   Just look at the state of your bedroom! Rupinda's mother shouted.
   It's not my fault, replied Rupinda.
   How did it get into such a mess? her mother asked.
   Hari did it when he was in a mood, Rupinda answered.

2 Add two more things Rupinda and her mother might say.

Thinking it through

1 Write about an argument Rupinda and her brother, Hari had. Include plenty of dialogue in it. (Use copymaster 1.)

2 Write a short story about Rupinda and Hari. Include some dialogue in it. Imagine that they are having great fun messing about in the garden, getting very muddy. Their father comes out and sees the mess. How does he react? What does he say?

Stepping Stones to help you

- Use 'speech bubbles' if your story is in pictures.
- Use 'speech marks' if you are writing a story.
- Put the words a person actually says inside the speech marks.
- Always begin a new line when someone new begins to speak.
(Use copymaster A.)

UNIT 2   Writing about Settings

Think ahead

All stories have a 'setting', where they take place. A good description of the setting helps the person reading your story build up a good picture in his/her mind. Read this beginning of a story. What setting is being described in it?

In the middle of a town by a river there was once a little park, not much bigger than somebody's front garden. It was all paved with brick, and in the centre of it grew a weeping willow tree. Around the edge of the park stood a row of red geraniums in pots. Along one side, beyond a white railing, flowed the green river, breaking into foamy ripples and waves in its hurry, sometimes throwing up sudden bursts of bubbles. And at each corner of the little park, facing inwards so they could see one another comfortably, crouched four stone lions. One had moss growing on its tail. One had a swallow's nest of straw built between its ears. One had a broken paw, where a boy had thrown a brick. And somebody had written I LOVE FRANK on the fourth lion. But the word FRANK, down by his tail, had been nearly washed off by rain, and the word 'I' was tangled up in his mane, so that if you glanced quickly, the lion seemed to have been labelled LOVE.

The four lions talked to each other all day long, without making a sound.

From *Tale of a One Way Street* by Joan Aitken

6

Thinking back

1 Where was the park?
2 What grew in its centre?
3 What stood round its edge?
4 What flowed along one side of the park?
5 What stood at each corner of the park?
6 Describe one of the lions in the park.

Thinking about it

Write a description of somewhere you know well, like your house, classroom or local park. Begin something like this:

It was a cold, winter day when I first visited _____ .

As I approached I _____

(Use copymaster 2.)

Thinking it through

Write the setting for the beginning of a story.
- Think of a door. Is it old or new? What is it made of?
- What sort of building does it belong to? a house? a cottage? a castle? a space ship?
- How do you open the door? with a key? handle?
- When your door is opened, what lies behind it? a passage way? a secret garden? a dark cellar? What do you see? How do you feel? What happens?

Stepping Stones to help you

- Are you going to write about a familiar setting or an imaginary one?
- Try to picture it in your mind.
- List some things you see, hear, smell and feel.
- Use interesting words to make the description come 'alive'.
(Use copymaster B.)

UNIT 3   Getting off to a Good Start

Think ahead

The way we begin a story is very important. How successful do you think these story starters are? Why?

I wanted to start my story in an attractive setting.

1 The thatched cottage stood in the clearing, in a sea of wild rose bushes which seemed to tumble everywhere around its windows and doors. The air was filled with the humming of bees. Giant pine trees lifted their heads to the heavens. In the background towered huge, snow-capped mountains.

I wanted to create a feeling of suspense.

2 CRRAACCKK! CRRUUNNCCHH! The metallic clinking noise stopped suddenly – then – silence. All Jed could hear was the wild thumping of his heart as it thudded in his ears. An eerie whirring noise started, as if something was trying to track Jed down. What was it? What was it coming from? What was going on? The whirring noise was getting louder, coming closer, approaching …

I wanted to create a feeling of gloom.

3 Big, black clouds filled the sky. It was dull and dreary – and it was drizzling. Sara felt damp and depressed as she lifted the tent flap and surveyed her soggy, rain-soaked surroundings. She sighed sadly to herself.

(See copymaster 3.)

Thinking back

1 The first story starter:
  a) How do you feel when you read it? Say why.
  b) Write what you know about the cottage.
  c) What sound was there to show it was in the summer?
  d) What adjectives describe the pine trees and mountains?
2 The second story starter:
  a) How do you feel when you read it? Say why.
  b) What sounds does Jed hear?
  c) Does Jed ever see what is coming?
  d) Copy one sentence you particularly like and say why.
3 The third story starter:
  a) How do you feel when you read it? Say why.
  b) This third story starter uses 'alliteration'. This is when many of the words used begin with the same letter (such as 'big, black'). Find other words like these which use alliteration in this story starter.

Thinking about it

1 Continue one of the story starters on the opposite page. What do you think happens next? Write a paragraph.
2 Look at copymaster 3. Then:
  a) Say whether you think each story starter was successful or not and explain why.
  b) Choose one of the story starters and continue the story. Write what you think happens next.

Thinking it through

Imagine you had just landed on an unexplored planet. You set out to discover what's out there. What do you see? hear? feel? Write an opening paragraph for a story. Try to use some words which build up a feeling that something exciting or unexpected is going to happen. Stop at a dramatic point. Don't give away too much! Leave the reader wanting to know more!

UNIT 4   Writing a Poem

Think ahead

This poem shows we can each think about the same thing in different ways. The poem is about two different people's views on water. Which point of view do you agree with?

Water's for ... washing, drinking
              making tea,
              cleaning the bath
              or scrubbing me;
              shining a car
              or rinsing a shirt
              watering tomatoes,
              shifting the dirt
                  ... my mum says.

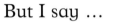

But I say ...   paddling in wellies
                 or just in feet
                 (puddles are good
                 but sea's a treat)
                 squirting at brothers,
                 splashing at Dad,
                 soaking my sister
                 to make her mad!
                 Mixing with mud
                 to bake a pie,
                 spraying the dog
                 or catching a fly.
                 Bath or puddle,
                 sleet or rain,
                 let's all play
                 a WATER game!

From *Water's for ...* by Judith Nicholls

Thinking back

1 List three things Mum says water is for in the poem.
2 List three things the poet says water is for.

Thinking about it

1 Make up your own poem about bath-time. It does not have to rhyme. Set it out like this:

My mum thinks bath-time is for … cleaning my ears, washing my hair,	I think bath-time is for … making bubbles,

2 Make up a number poem about ten things you see or do in a day. Try to make it rhyme. Do it like this:
   One, one, see the rising sun.
   Two, two, walk in morning dew.
(Use copymaster 4.)

Thinking it through

1 List as many different types of weather as you can.
   Say what you think each type of weather is like. Do it like this:
   The sun burns like a builder's blowlamp.
2 Write a poem about the sorts of weather we have in each season. Do it like this:
   Winter sometimes brings the snow,
   And icy winds that blow and blow.

Stepping Stones to help you

• Jot your ideas down in rough.
• Choose your best ideas and experiment with them.
• When you are happy, make a best copy.
(Use copymaster C.)

UNIT 5   Calligrams and Shape Poems

Think ahead

A 'calligram' is a single word whose shape, or the way in which it is written, makes you think of its meaning.

A 'shape poem' is a list of words, thoughts or ideas which are presented in a particular way or shape to remind you of the subject in some way.

Which of these are calligrams? Which are shape poems?

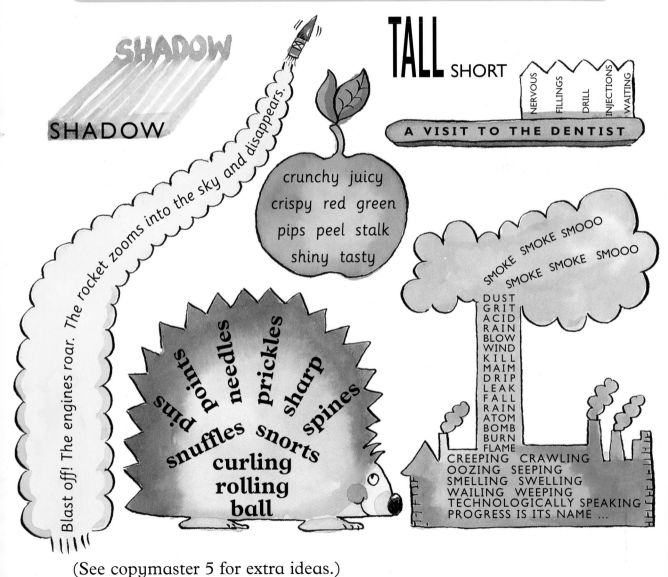

(See copymaster 5 for extra ideas.)

Thinking back

Choose one of these subjects:

a) television   b) carrot   c) snake   d) butterfly
- In rough, draw a large outline of your chosen object.
- In it write interesting words that describe the object.
- Check the spelling of the words.
- Make a best copy of your idea in your book.

Thinking about it

1 **Choose four of these words. Make interesting calligrams of them.**
   SHIVER   FIRE   GHOST   SCREAM
   FROG   SKYSCRAPER   LADDER   GUITAR
   - Experiment with your ideas in rough on a sheet of paper.
   - Try out different colours and writing tools.
   - When you are happy with your ideas, make a best copy in your book.
2 Make calligrams of four pairs of these words. Follow the same steps for doing them, as in 1) above.
   HOT – COLD   FAST – SLOW   FAT – THIN
   CLEAN – DIRTY   DARK – LIGHT   LOUD – SOFT

Thinking it through

Think of an interesting subject. Use some of these ideas to start you thinking:

SPAGHETTI   AEROPLANES   FIREWORKS   DINOSAURS
- In rough, write an interesting sentence or set of sentences about your subject.
- They may rhyme but they don't have to.
- Experiment with your ideas and turn them into a shape poem.
- When you are happy with your ideas, make a best copy in your book.

UNIT 6   Writing a Playscript

Think ahead

A play usually has two or more characters in it. Sometimes a storyteller or narrator is used in a play. What is their job?

Jack climbs the Beanstalk

NARRATOR	When he got to the top of the beanstalk, Jack saw a castle in the distance. Feeling a little nervous, he walked towards it, plucked up his courage and knocked on the huge door. When it opened, there stood a giant's wife, towering above him.
GIANT'S WIFE	What do you want, young man?
JACK	Sorry to bother you, but I've just climbed that tall beanstalk and I'm thirsty. May I have a drink, please?
GIANT'S WIFE	Yes, but you must be quick. You must not be here when my husband arrives.
JACK	Doesn't your husband like visitors?
GIANT'S WIFE	He likes them so much, he eats them!
NARRATOR	Jack was just about to move when suddenly the ground began to shake. BOOM! BOOM! BOOM!
JACK	What's that? Is it an earthquake?
GIANT'S WIFE	It's my husband. He has come home for his lunch. Come in and hide, quickly, before he sees you!

(Adapted from the story of *Jack and the Beanstalk*)

Thinking back

1 Who are the two main characters in this part of the play?
2 How can you tell every time a new character speaks?
3 What is the name of the story from which the play comes?
4 Name one other character that appears in the rest of the story.
5 What does the narrator do?
6 Write one thing   a) the giant's wife says   b) Jack says.

Thinking about it

1 Make up a playscript to tell the next part of the story. Give your scene a title. (Use copymaster 6.)
2 Use this plan to help you.
   – The giant's wife hides Jack in a cupboard.
   – The giant thinks he can smell a human being.
   – His wife takes his mind off this by bringing him his lunch.
   – After lunch the giant counts his money and falls asleep.
   – Jack grabs the money and runs for it as the giant wakes up.

Thinking it through

1 Write a playscript for the last part of the story called 'Jack escapes'.
2 Choose one of the opening scenes of the story, either 'Jack goes to market' or 'The magic beanstalk'. Write a playscript for one of these scenes.

Stepping Stones to help you

Characters
• Write the characters' names clearly.
• Start a new line each time a new character speaks.
Setting the scene
• Use a storyteller or narrator to introduce and tell parts of the story. (Use copymaster D.)

Think ahead

When we get information from books we don't need to write down everything. We can record the information on a chart or find the key words and use these as notes to help us remember. Some key words are in **bold** *below. Which other words would you put in* **bold**?

Some animals eat during the day and sleep at night.
Some do things the opposite way round.

A **fox** lives in a **den** (a hole in a bank) and hunts at **night**. It hunts for **small animals** and sometimes kills chickens on farms.

Another **night-time feeder** is the **badger**. It leaves its **sett** (its home) to look for **frogs** or **mice**.

Hedgehogs are also out at night searching for worms and slugs. They then return to their homes, perhaps an old rabbit burrow or a pile of old leaves.

Moles spend nearly all their time in their underground tunnels, where it is always dark, so they eat at any time of night or day!

On the other hand, squirrels make their nests (called dreys) in trees, and like to look for food in the light.

Rabbits prefer the light, too. They can be found outside their burrows, eating early in the morning or late afternoon.

Thinking back

Copy this chart in your book. Use the information opposite to help you. Put a tick (✓) or a cross (✗) in each box.

When it eats	Badger	Fox	Hedgehog	Mole	Rabbit	Squirrel
Day-time						
Night-time						

 Thinking about it

1 Write some sentences about each animal, based on information from this chart.

Where it lives	Badger	Fox	Hedgehog	Mole	Rabbit	Squirrel
Above ground			✓			✓
Below ground	✓	✓		✓	✓	

2 Write five questions for a friend to answer, based on the chart. For example: Where does a mole live?
3 Write the name given to the home of each animal.

 Thinking it through

1 Here are some key words about the food some animals eat.
badger: meat – frogs, mice and toads
fox: meat – birds, mice, rats, chickens (if they can catch them)
hedgehog: insects – slugs and snails
Write some sentences about each animal.
2 Copy these sentences. Underline the key words in them.
A mole has a similar diet to a hedgehog. It too, eats insects, snails and slugs. It also likes worms.
Rabbits eat any green food, such as grass, young shoots, as well as plants such as cabbages, sprouts and lettuces.
Squirrels look for food on the ground as well as in trees. They will eat birds' eggs, nuts and green shoots.
(Use copymaster 7.)

UNIT 8   Writing a Report

Think ahead

Ben's teacher asked him to write a report about his pet. First of all he started by jotting down some notes in the form of a web diagram. He organised his notes under different headings. Do you think this was a sensible way to work? Why? What sort of notes might he have written under the other headings in the boxes below?

Advantages and disadvantages

Appearance
Small, white, wiry hair, cheeky, black eyes, sticking-up ears, short legs, strong teeth

A typical day for my pet

My pet

Exercise
Needs lots of exercise, often plays in garden, needs long walk every day, doesn't matter about weather.

Equipment needed

Food
One main meal a day, meat, dog biscuits, plenty of water, for a treat give a few chocolate drops.

Here is the start of Ben's report:

My pet

Introduction
I have a pet dog. Her name is Wags.
She is a West Highland Terrier.

Appearance
Wags is a small white dog, with short, wiry hair. She is quite cheeky-looking, with alert, black eyes. Her ears stick up and always make her look inquisitive. Wags has short strong legs, and sharp, strong teeth.

Thinking back

What do you think Ben wrote about the exercise Wags needs?
Use his notes to help you write a paragraph on this subject.
Do it in rough first and then check it for spelling and punctuation
to make sure it makes sense.
Remember to give your paragraph a heading.
When you are happy, make a best copy.

Thinking about it

Plan and write a report on a pet you have (or would like to have).
Use Ben's headings to help you write your notes. (Use
copymaster 8.)
When you have written your notes, write a draft report in rough
or on the computer.
Read it through for mistakes ('proof-read' it) and then write a
best copy.

Thinking it through

Choose an animal you know something about, or would like to
know about.
Use a reference book to help you if you need more information.
Write a report on the animal of your choice.
Use the Stepping Stones to help you write your report.

Stepping Stones to help you

- Write notes on all you know, or can find out, about the subject.
- Organise your notes under suitable headings.
- Write your report in rough first.
- Write a few sentences for each heading.
- 'Proof-read' your draft for mistakes, then write the final copy of
  your report.

(Use copymaster E.)

UNIT 9   Key Events

Think ahead

All stories are made up of a series of events that happen. It is helpful to list the most important events when you are planning a story. What ways are used to record the key events of the story below?

1. Mouse wakes lion. Lion angry.

2. Mouse begs lion to let him go.

3. Later, lion gets caught in hunter's net.

4. Mouse gnaws through ropes of net.

5. Lion escapes.

6. Lion and mouse become good friends.

Thinking back

Write a simple story based on the pictures and notes on the opposite page. Begin like this:

> One day, a mouse walked over the paw of a sleeping lion. The lion woke up. He was very angry at the mouse for waking him up. He roared loudly at the poor mouse.

Thinking about it

1 Here are the key events from another fable, in note form. Make a storyboard. Draw a simple picture to show each event. Write the notes under each picture.
  - Very hot day. Crow thirsty.
  - Crow sees jug containing water.
  - Crow tries to drink water. Beak too short. Can't reach.
  - Has idea. Picks up stones in beak.
  - Drops stones in jug. Raises level of water.
  - Now crow is able to drink.
2 Now write a simple story based on your storyboard.

Thinking it through

List the main events, or make a storyboard, of any fable you know well: for example, The Hare and the Tortoise, The Boy Who Cried Wolf, The North Wind and the Sun, The Town Mouse and the Country Mouse.
(Use copymaster 9.)

Writing about Characters

Think ahead

Every story must have at least one main character. Read this description of the Nurgla. How does the author use interesting phrases and words to describe the Nurgla's appearance?

The Nurgla was very, very old, and very, very tired, and he looked as old and tired as he felt. His small head was wrinkled and lined with age; the two leathery horns which sprouted from the top of his forehead were crumpled and creased; and an untidy fringe of green, seaweed-like hair hung over his eyebrows and sometimes made him furious because it got in his eyes. Two large nostrils flared in the folds of his craggy cheeks, and dreadful sharp teeth jutted out from his huge jaws. A ridge of jagged spikes ran the length of the Nurgla's long, long neck, down the spine of his enormous body, right to the very tip of his scaly tail. To complete the horrible picture, his round body was covered in hard, overlapping, armour-like plates, and his vast flippers were an unbelievable size eighteen. In short, the Nurgla was hideous.

From *Katy and the Nurgla* by Harry Secombe

Thinking back

1 **Copy and complete these facts about the Nurgla.**
   a) The Nurgla has a _____ head with two _____ horns.
   b) His hair is _____ and _____ .
   c) The Nurgla has _____ jaws with _____ teeth.
   d) The Nurgla has a _____ body and a _____ tail.
   e) Down his back he has a ridge of _____ spikes.
2 Write two more facts about the Nurgla that have been missed out.

Thinking about it

1 What sort of things do you think the Nurgla does? Make up five sentences about things you think it does. For example, does it eat very greedily? snore loudly? Does it jump out and frighten people?
2 How does the Nurgla speak? For example, does it: roar noisily? speak politely? whisper? What sort of things does it say? Write down your ideas.

Thinking it through

1 Make up your own scary monster. Write a description of it, like the description of the Nurgla.
   (Use copymaster 10.)
2 Think of a person you know very well. For example, it could be a friend or a teacher. Write a description of him or her.

Stepping Stones to help you

- When describing characters write about:
  their appearance   things they do and say
  other interesting facts
- Use good describing words.
(Use copymaster F.)

UNIT 11   Planning a Story

Think ahead

When you plan a story remember that all stories have three main ingredients: characters (who the story is about); a setting (where the story takes place); a series of events (things that happen).
Who are the main characters in the story below?

Long ago in China, the sun played a trick on the people. It got so hot that nothing grew and all the seas began to dry up.

Yang, who was a good archer, had an idea. He aimed an arrow at the sun and fired: THWANG! When the sun saw this it got scared and hid behind a mountain. For days there was darkness. The people cried out to the sun to come out. They promised it that it would not be harmed. But it was no good. There it stayed and would not come out.

"Perhaps it cannot hear us," they said. "We need a louder voice." So they fetched a lion.

"GRRRRR," it roared. But its roar was so frightening, the sun refused to come out.

"A cow has a loud voice, but it is less frightening than a lion's roar," they said. So they fetched a cow.

"Moooooo," said the cow. But the sun was still afraid.

"How about a cock?" someone said. So they fetched a cock.

"Cock-a-doodle-doo," it crowed. Now the sun liked this sound. Indeed, it was so curious to find out what was making the noise, that it peeked out from behind the mountain. The people were so happy that they cheered and the sun realised it was safe to come out. Ever since that time the sun has never been afraid to come out when it hears the cock crow and has never played another trick on the people.

(Adapted from a Chinese myth)

Thinking back

Write these key events from the story opposite in the correct order.
- Long ago, the sun got so hot nothing grew.
- They got a cow to moo but it was also too loud.
- Yang fired at the sun with his bow and arrow.
- When the cock crowed the sun decided to come out.
- The sun hid behind a mountain.
- They got a lion to roar but it was too loud.
- The people tried calling the sun but it pretended not to hear.

 Thinking about it

Use copymaster 11 to help you write a plan of the story.

 Thinking it through

Make up your own story.
- Instead of the sun playing tricks, why not have some other form of weather? (For example, the moon, thunder, rain.)
- Instead of Yang using a bow and arrow why not have someone else using a net? a fishing rod? something else?
- Instead of hiding behind a mountain, what else could be used as a hiding place?
- Why not change some of the animals used?
- Use your story planner (copymaster 11) to help you.

Stepping Stones to help you

- Who are the main characters? What are they like?
- Where does the story take place?
- How does the story begin?
- What problem or problems are there?
- How does the story end?
(Use copymaster G.)

UNIT 12 Writing a Story Sequel

Think ahead

A 'story sequel' is when we begin with a familiar story, and then write another story in which the characters stay the same, but we change the events of the story. Here, we begin with a well-known story. How does it usually end?

Once upon a time there were three Billy Goats Gruff. There was Big Billy Goat Gruff, Middle-size Billy Goat Gruff and Little Billy Goat Gruff. They lived on one side of a river. Over the river was a wooden bridge. Under that wooden bridge lived an ugly troll. On the other side of the river there was a field of lovely, juicy, green grass.

One day, the Billy Goats Gruff decided to go across the bridge to eat the grass on the other side of the river. Little Billy Goat Gruff started to go across first. Trip-trap, trip-trap went his hoofs on the bridge.

Suddenly, the ugly troll jumped up from beneath the bridge. When he saw the Little Billy Goat Gruff, the troll roared, "I'm a troll, fol-di-roll and I'll eat you up for my supper!"

The Little Billy Goat Gruff was frightened but said in a trembling voice, "Please Mr Troll, please don't eat me. Why don't you wait for my brother, Middle-size Billy Goat Gruff? He's bigger and juicier than me."

"Very well," roared the troll. "I will." He let the Little Billy Goat Gruff pass across the bridge and into the field with the lovely, green, juicy grass.

Thinking back

In your book, write the usual ending to the story of the Billy Goats Gruff in your own words. Make it end so that the Billy Goats live happily ever after! (Use copymaster 12.)

 Thinking about it

Change the ending of the story. Make up your own ending. Think of something very different that could happen. Here are two suggestions (or use your own ideas):
– Allow the Troll to win. How does he do it? What happens?
– Have the Billy Goats Gruff make friends with the Troll and give the story an even happier ending! What do the goats say and do to persuade the Troll to be their friend? What sort of things do they do together?

 Thinking it through

1 Make up and write a sequel to the story. Use the same characters and the same idea of the goats trying to outsmart the Troll. Choose one of the following:
   – Think of *other* ways the goats could have got across the river. The Troll tries in vain to get them, but doesn't succeed. Write what happens.
   – Change the setting. This time the goats have to try to get past the Troll's cave to get to the juicy grass. What happens?
   – Imagine that the Troll manages to survive when he gets butted into the water. He sneaks back under the bridge. When the goats try to pass over the bridge on their way back, he is ready for them! What has he got planned? Does he get the goats or do they get past him again? What happens?
2 Make up a different ending for another well-known traditional tale: for example, Goldilocks, Jack and the Beanstalk, The Gingerbread Man, Little Red Riding Hood.

Performance Poetry

What do you think a 'performance poem' is?

Try reading this poem together.
Tap out the rhythm as you do so.
Does each verse have the same rhythm?
Does the poem rhyme? How?

Going Through the Old Photos

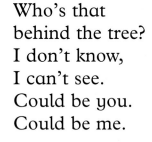

Who's that?
That's your Auntie Mabel
and that's me
under the table.

Who's that?
That's Uncle Billy.
Who's that?
Me being silly.

Who's that
licking a lolly?
I'm not sure
but I think it's Polly.

Who's that
behind the tree?
I don't know,
I can't see.
Could be you.
Could be me.

Who's that?
Baby Joe.
Who's that?
I don't know.

Who's that standing
on his head?
Turn it round.
It's Uncle Ted.

From *Going Through the Old Photos* by Michael Rosen

28

Thinking back

Answer these questions.
1 The poem was called 'Going Through the Old _____'.
2 There is a photo of Auntie _____ .
3 There is a photo of Uncle _____ and Uncle _____ .
4 Polly was licking a _____ .
5 There is a photo of Baby _____ .
6 It isn't possible to see who is behind the _____ .
7 Uncle Ted was standing on his _____ .
8 There are _____ verses in the poem.

 Thinking about it

Copy these verses and think of a way to finish them off.

1 Who's that?
  It's Uncle Burt.
  What's he wearing?

  _____

2 Who's that?
  It's Auntie Lil.
  She really looks

  _____

3 Who's that?
  It's me at school.

  _____

  _____

4 Who's that?
  It's Tibs, the cat.

  _____

  _____

Thinking it through

1 Make up four more verses of your own.
2 Make up your own version of the 'Monday's Child' poem.
(Use copymaster 13.)

29

UNIT 14   Writing Instructions

Think ahead

When we write instructions it is important to put in a 'what you will need' section. Why?

How to write a Secret Message

What you need:

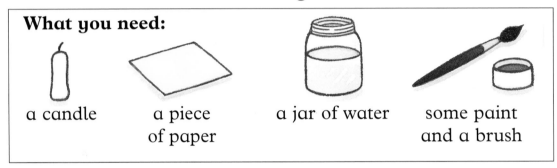

a candle   a piece
             of paper   a jar of water   some paint
                                             and a brush

What you do:

1
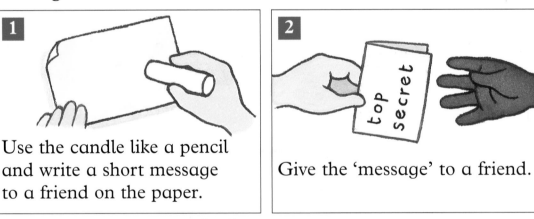

Use the candle like a pencil
and write a short message
to a friend on the paper.

2

Give the 'message' to a friend.

3

Paint over the paper with a
thin 'wash' of watery paint.

4

meet me
at 5 o'clock

Read the message that
appears.

Thinking back

1 What are the instructions for?
2 List the things you need. Copy and complete this sentence:
   To write a secret message, you need a candle ...
3 How many steps are there altogether?
4 Why is it helpful to have numbered steps?
5 Why is it helpful to have pictures?

Thinking about it

Here is a recipe for currant buns. Copy it out so it is easier to read. (Use copymaster 14 to help you.)
   You need: 100 g of margarine, 100 g of caster sugar, 200 g of self-raising flour, 150 g of sultanas, ½ teaspoon of mixed spice, a pinch of salt and a little milk. Put all the dry ingredients into a bowl. Pour in the milk. Stir until the mixture is smooth and firm. Form the mixture into small balls. Put the balls onto a greased baking tray. Pop the tray into a hot oven and cook for 12 minutes.

Thinking it through

1 Write the instructions for either: a) making a jam sandwich or b) washing your hair. (Use copymaster 14.)
2 Write how to play noughts and crosses. Use the following headings:
   – Aim of the game   – Number of players
   – Equipment needed   – Rules of the game

Stepping Stones to help you

• Write the aim first.
• Next write what is needed.
• Write clear steps on what you have to do.
(Use copymaster H.)

We don't always need to write everything *down. Sometimes we can just write notes. When we write notes we only write down the most important words. Can you think of times when we could use notes?*

Here is some information on dinosaurs that I found in an encyclopaedia.

Stegosaurus This dinosaur lived on dry land. It was a plant-eater and grew up to nine metres in length. Its body was protected by a thick skin like armour. Its back was protected by two rows of bony plates. Stegosaurus had two pairs of spikes at the end of its tail with which to defend itself.

Tyrannosaurus Rex This dinosaur was known as the 'king of dinosaurs'. (The word 'Rex' actually means 'king' in Latin.) Tyrannosaurus was the biggest, fiercest, flesh-eating dinosaur that ever lived. Tyrannosaurus grew to a length of 14 metres. It was as long as a bus. It walked upright on its two strong back legs. Its feet had sharp, terrifying claws. Its front legs were shorter. Its huge jaws contained great, sharp teeth which grew 15 centimetres long.

Here are some notes I wrote about Tyrannosaurus.

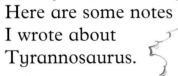

Tyrannosaurus Rex – known as 'king of dinosaurs' – 'Rex' means 'king' – biggest, fiercest, flesh-eating dinosaur – length 14 metres – walked upright on powerful back legs – sharp claws – shorter front legs – great, sharp teeth, 15 centimetres long

Thinking back

1 Copy the information about Stegosaurus. Underline only the important words. Do it like this:

This dinosaur <u>lived on dry land</u>. It was a <u>plant-eater</u> and grew up to <u>nine metres in length</u>.

2 Here are some notes on a dinosaur called Deinonychus. Write out the notes in proper sentences

flesh-eater – walked on back legs – big claw on each foot – short front legs – only 3 metres – strong – able to overpower bigger dinosaurs – could run fast – ran with long tail stretched out straight.

 Thinking about it

Write an accurate description of both dinosaurs in note form. Do it like this:

Tyrannosaurus: stands upright on two powerful back legs – feet have three claws at front, one claw at back – two front legs much shorter and thinner

 Thinking it through

Notes are useful when planning ahead, to help you organise your ideas. Imagine you are going on a school visit to the Natural History Museum. Make some notes.

– What will you wear? (Remember you can't rely on the weather!)
– What will you eat? (packed lunch, snacks, anything else?)
– What else will you take with you? (games, books and other things for the journey; things you will need at the museum, such as notebook, camera.)
– List five things you would like to find out about dinosaurs whilst you are there.

(Use copymaster 15.)

UNIT 16　What Would *You* Do?

Think ahead

A good author makes you, the reader, feel part of the story, as if you were actually there. How would you feel if you were Barney? What would you be thinking? What would you do next?

(Barney had slipped and fallen to the bottom of the pit, which was used as a dump.)

Barney lay with his eyes shut, waiting for his thoughts to stop being mixed up. Then he opened them. He was lying in a kind of shelter. Looking up he could see a roof, or part of a roof, made of elder branches, a very rotten old carpet, and rusty old sheets of iron. There was a big hole, through which he must have fallen. He could see the white walls of the cliff, the trees and creepers at the top, and the sky with clouds passing over it.

Barney decided he wasn't dead. He didn't even seem to be very much hurt. He turned his head and looked around him. It was dark in this den after looking at the white chalk, and he couldn't see what sort of place it was. It seemed to be partly a cave dug into the chalk, partly a shelter built out over the mouth of the cave. There was a cool, damp smell. Woodlice and earwigs dropped from the roof where he had broken through it.

He lay quiet and looked around the cave again. Now that his eyes were used to it he could see further into the dark part of the cave.

There was somebody there!

From *Stig of the Dump* by Clive King

Thinking back

1 Who is the passage about?
2 What has happened?
3 Rewrite the first paragraph in the first person, as if it had happened to you. Do it like this:

   I lay with my eyes shut, waiting for my thoughts to stop being mixed up.

Thinking about it

1 Write some of the thoughts and feelings that might have been going through your head if you were Barney as you tried to work out where you were and what sort of a place you had landed yourself in. Here are some ideas to start you off:

   I wish my head would stop spinning. I hope I haven't broken anything. Where am I? What a strange place this is!
2 Imagine what happens next. Write it in the first person as if it happened to you. (If possible, find out what really happened in the actual book!)

Thinking it through

Write what you think happened just before the passage in the book. Write it in the first person as if you are Barney. Here are some things to think about to help you:

- Where was Barney when he had slipped?
- Who used the pit as a dump?
- What had Barney been doing near the edge of the pit in the first place?
- How had he slipped – or had he been pushed?
- Was he with anyone else or on his own?

(Use copymaster 16.)

Think ahead

Many stories are written in chapters. What is a chapter? Here is one chapter of a longer story. Read it and then say what you think the other chapters could be about.

The high stone walls of the Castle of Doom loomed above them. Little John reached the top of the wall and scrambled over the battlements. He could hear soldiers laughing and joking in the guardhouse below, but there was no guard on duty. Little John beckoned to the others to climb up the rope whilst it was all clear.

Soon, all three of them, Little John, Braveheart and Midge, were all safely inside the castle. Then, as a dark cloud covered the moon, they headed towards the dungeons, where Princess Petronella was held prisoner.

They crept across the courtyard, past the guards' room. They froze in the shadows as one guard came out and walked towards the main hall. Little John gulped with relief when he had passed.

Finally they reached the door to the dungeons. Midge opened it and stuck out his tongue at the astonished guard inside. The soldier leapt to his feet and chased after Midge, tripping over Braveheart's outstretched leg as he did so. Little John quickly gagged and bound him. They then unlocked the jail door, waking the Princess with a start. She smiled with delight when she saw them and realised they had come to rescue her.

Peering carefully around to make sure no-one had heard them, the group, including Princess Petronella, crept quietly towards the castle gate … and freedom!

Thinking back

1 Write down the main series of events in the story, like this:
   Princess Petronella is being held captive at the Castle of Doom.
   Little John, Braveheart and Midge set out to rescue her.
2 Where is the story set?
3 Describe what you think the Castle of Doom is like.
4 Who are the main characters in the story?
5 Write a character profile of one of the characters. (See unit 10.)

 Thinking about it

Imagine that the Duke of Darkness, who lives in the Castle of Doom, has stolen a magic sword. Anyone who uses the sword cannot be harmed. Little John, Braveheart, Midge and the Princess set out to get the sword back. Write about how they do it. You can make some other things happen whilst inside the castle to make it more exciting – but the group must succeed in their mission! Plan your ideas in rough first.

 Thinking it through

Use what you wrote in the 'Thinking about it' section as the first chapter of a longer story. Use the ideas on copymaster 17 to help you draft, review, edit and write some other chapters.
(Why not ask other children to write some of the chapters? You could then put your chapters together and make one long book.)

Stepping Stones to help you

- Does your story make sense?
- Is it interesting enough?
- Have you described the characters and settings well enough?
- Have you used dialogue effectively?
(Use copymaster I.)

UNIT 18   Writing a Book Review

Think ahead

When you have read a book you have enjoyed it is helpful to write a review of it, to recommend it to others. What sort of things would you put in a book review?

The children in Asif's class recommend books to each other. Here is a review Asif wrote about a book he liked.

If you want excitement, tension and drama then read 'The Iron Man' by Ted Hughes. I couldn't stop reading it once I had started. It was scary and exciting at the same time! You never quite knew what would happen next.

The two characters I liked best were Hogarth, a farmer's son, and the Iron Man. In the book, Hogarth is very brave. He makes friends with the Iron Man.

The story takes place in farming country, near the sea, and is about how the Iron Man appears and saves the world. The bit I enjoyed best was when the family was having a picnic and the Iron Man's fist came up through the ground, and terrified them!

Ted Hughes uses some good words to build up the drama and the tension. The book has a really good ending but I won't tell you about it or that would spoil it!

I am looking forward to reading its sequel, called 'The Iron Woman'. I give this book ten out of ten and recommend it to you. Don't miss it!

Book reviewer: Asif

Thinking back

1 What was the name of the book?
2 Who was the author?
3 Name two characters from the book.
4 Where does the story take place?
5 What happens in the book?
6 What words does Asif use to describe the book?
7 What is the sequel to the book called?
8 a) Who wrote the book review? b) Who was he writing it for?

 Thinking about it

Write a book review of a book you have just recently read and
enjoyed. Use copymaster 18 to help you. Give your review to
a friend to read.

 Thinking it through

Write about a book you have just read. Choose from the
following suggestions.
Write a rough draft first.
a) In under 50 words write a book blurb for the back of the book.
b) Design a new front cover for the book.
c) Write a character profile for your favourite character.
d) Design a poster, like Asif's, to persuade other children to read
   the book.

Stepping Stones to help you

• Give the title and author.
• Give your opinion of some of the characters.
• Say where the story is set and something about what happens.
• Write what you think of the author's style and use of language.
(Use copymaster J.)

Think ahead

Poems often use sounds to create effects. Some poems use 'alliteration' where lots of words begin with the same letter. Some poems use 'onomatopoeia' where lots of words are used that describe the sounds of things. Which poem below uses a) mainly alliteration? b) mainly onomatopoeia?

Lucy Lane likes ...

Lucy Lane loves licking
   lollipops,
But Sharon Sharp loves
   going to the shops.
Dan Diprose loves
   digging drains,
But Tracy Tomms likes
   travelling on trains.

Metal fettle

The clank of a tank,
the chink of chains,
the tinkle of tins,
the rattle of trains.

The click of a clasp,
the clang of a bell,
the creak of a hinge,
the chime of a spell.

The shatter of cymbals,
the clash of swords,
the clatter of cutlery,
the twang of chords.

The ping of keys,
the song of a wheel,
the plink of pans,
the ring of steel.

'Metal fettle' by John Rice from
Bears Don't Like Bananas

Thinking back

1 Copy the first poem. Underline all the first letters of words that sound the same. Do it like this:

  <u>L</u>ucy <u>L</u>ane <u>l</u>oves <u>l</u>icking <u>l</u>ollipops.

2 Write all the 'sound' words (such as clank) from the second poem.

Thinking about it

1 a) Write ten people's names and then add an adjective beginning with the same letter (such as Beautiful Betty).
  b) Write what each person might like, such as Beautiful Betty likes buttered buns with beans and beetroot. (Write a rough draft of your ideas first. Your poem does not have to rhyme.)

2 Draw a large outline of an open mouth on a piece of paper. In it write all the sounds mouths can make, such as shout, whisper, mumble, talk.

Thinking it through

Take one of the following themes: in the kitchen; musical instruments; noises at night; traffic; the farm; the jungle. Make up a poem using as many sound words as possible, linked to your theme, such as 'Cars screech and hoot, buses rattle and growl, lorries thunder and judder, scooters pop pop.' Set it out like the 'Metal fettle' poem opposite. (Do a rough draft first. Use the Stepping Stones below to help you.)

Stepping Stones to help you

- Jot your ideas down in rough.
- Choose your best ideas and experiment with them.
- When you are happy, make a best copy.
(Use copymaster C.)

UNIT 20 Writing a Letter

Have you ever thought of writing to your favourite author or poet? Authors like receiving letters from children who have enjoyed their work. Who is the letter below written to? Have you read any of his poems or books?

14 Summerfield Close,
Luton,
LU2 8RX.
5th March

Dear Mr Milligan,

I am writing to tell you how much I enjoy reading your poems. My favourite poem is 'The Ning Nang Nong'. I like it especially because of the way it plays with words and sounds. It makes me smile when I read about tea pots that go 'jibber jabber joo' and cows that go 'bong'! In class we have fun saying it aloud because it's a bit of a tongue-twister in places.

One of your poems that really makes me sad, though, is 'The Dog Lovers', about a family who buy a dog without really thinking. They don't look after it properly and it escapes and gets run over. We have a pet dog called Smudge. She's just like a member of our family. People shouldn't have dogs if they are not prepared to love them, care for them and take them for walks.

Please keep writing poems.

Love from

Ian Fuller

Thinking back

1 Who is the letter to?
2 Who is the letter from?
3 Why is Ian writing to this author?
4 Which two poems are mentioned?
5 How many paragraphs does the letter have?
6 Draw a rectangle 12 cm by 15 cm in your book. Write your name and address in it, as if you were addressing an envelope to yourself. Punctuate it correctly.

Thinking about it

Think of an author you would like to write to. You can address it to the publisher, whose address you will find inside the book. Use Ian's letter to help you set it out correctly. Divide it into two main paragraphs. In the first paragraph say what you liked about a specific story or poem. In the second paragraph give the author some news or information about yourself.
(Use copymaster 20.)

Thinking it through

Write a letter to someone connected with school (your teacher, head teacher, caretaker, secretary, cook, lollipop lady). Divide it into two paragraphs. In the first, thank them for the things they do for you or for one specific thing. In the second paragraph, ask them a question about some aspect of their job.

Stepping Stones to help you

- Think carefully about who it is to. (It will affect what you write and how you write it.)
- Set it out correctly (see Ian's letter opposite).
- Divide it into paragraphs.
(Use copymaster K.)

UNIT 21   Recounting Events

Think ahead

The same event may be recounted in many different ways – as a story, as a report, in the form of a letter and so on. In what form is the event below recounted?

At last the day everyone had been waiting for had arrived. People stood on balconies, crowded at windows and waited at barriers. The streets were festooned with bunting and children clutched flags.

Humpty Dumpty made himself comfortable on a high wall overlooking the square. He had a great view.

Suddenly there was an excited murmur of "They're coming! I can see them!"

Humpty strained to see. In his excitement he leaned forward expectantly. As he did so, he lost his balance. Frantically Humpty tried to grab the top of the wall – but it was no use. He toppled forward and let out a yell as he plunged downwards. Humpty hit the pavement. His shell cracked into a thousand pieces.

The soldier leading the parade caught sight of Humpty falling and rushed forward to help. The crowds pulled back to make way as the rest of the soldiers joined in. In spite of their expert knowledge, all the king's horses and all the king's men couldn't put Humpty together again. It was a very sad end to what should have been a happy day.

Thinking back

1 Who are the main characters in the story?
2 Where is the story set?
3 What are the main events in the story?
4 Write the nursery rhyme on which the story is based.

Thinking about it

Imagine you are a reporter at the scene. Write a newspaper article about the event. Think of a good headline. Set the scene with a few facts. Report what some eyewitnesses say they saw. For example, a bystander, a soldier, a doctor at the hospital. Draw a picture to go with your report. (You could use a computer to help you set out your report.)
(Use copymaster 21.)

Thinking it through

1 Imagine you were the soldier leading the parade. Write a letter to your mother recounting the incident. Here are some ideas. Begin like this:

> The Royal Barracks
> The King's Palace.
>
> Dear Mum,
>   I hope everyone at home is well.
>   I am just writing to tell you about a strange event that happened last week.

Next, write a paragraph of a few sentences setting the scene. Then write a paragraph about the actual accident and the part you took in the whole event.
Finally finish off the letter with other news.
2 Take another nursery rhyme, such as Jack and Jill, Doctor Foster, Hey Diddle, Diddle. Recount the same event either as a story, a news report or in the form of a letter.

UNIT 22 Alphabetically-ordered Texts

Think ahead

Lots of books are organised into alphabetical order, such as encyclopaedias and dictionaries. Can you name any more? Tara has visited a building site and has made an alphabetical list of some things she saw there. Which word has she got in the wrong order?

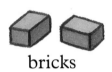

bricks

A brick is a block of hard-baked clay, used for building walls.

cables

These are lengths of wire with a plastic coating, used to carry electricity.

cement

This is a grey powder which is mixed with sand and water. It hardens when dry. It is used to stick bricks together.

glass

Glass is a hard, transparent material used for windows. It breaks easily. You can get 'frosted' glass which is opaque (not transparent).

guttering

Guttering, and drain pipes, are usually made from plastic. They carry rain water away from buildings.

sand

Sand is small grains of rock. Builders use sand a lot. It is one of the things cement is made from.

timber

Timber is another name for wood. It is used a lot in buildings for making things like frames, floors, roofs.

tiles

A tile is a flat piece of baked clay used for putting on the roof of a house.

Thinking back

1 What is an alphabetical order?
2 Why do we put things in alphabetical order?
3 In Tara's list which word comes
   a) first   b) after glass?   c) before cement?
4 What is sand?
5 What is cement used for?
6 If Tara had put breeze blocks in her list where would they have come?

Thinking about it

Tara also discovered the names of some tools that builders use. Find out what they are used for and write a definition for each. Write them out in an alphabetically-ordered list, with their definitions, like the one opposite.

saw	hammer	screwdriver	awl	drill
sandpaper	spirit level	chisel	knife	pliers

(Use copymaster 22.)

Thinking it through

1 Find out what each of the buildings below is used for and write a sentence about each one. Write their names and definitions in alphabetical order.

museum	bungalow	castle	abbey	factory
hangar	cathedral	hospital	palace	barn

2 Write an alphabet of people. Think of the name of a job beginning with each letter of the alphabet. For example, A is for astronaut; B is for baker, and so on. (You might not be able to think of jobs for one or two letters.)
3 Try writing an alphabet of animals or countries in the same way.